T0023976

STICKER ART PUZZLES

THUNDER BAY
P · R · E · S · S
San Diego, California

Thunder Bay Press
An imprint of Printers Row Publishing Group
9717 Pacific Heights Blvd., San Diego, CA 92121
www.thunderbaybooks.com • mail@thunderbaybooks.com

Printers Row Publishing Group is a division of Readerlink Distribution Services, LLC.
Thunder Bay Press is a registered trademark of Readerlink Distribution Services, LLC.

Correspondence regarding the content of this book should be sent to Thunder Bay Press,
Editorial Department, at the above address.

Thunder Bay Press
Publisher: Peter Norton
Associate Publisher: Ana Parker
Art Director: Charles McStravick
Senior Developmental Editor: Diane Cain
Senior Project Editor: Jessica Matteson
Production Team: Beno Chan, Rusty von Dyl

Produced by Judy O Productions, Inc.
Author: Gina Gold

ISBN: 978-1-64517-952-8

Printed, manufactured, and assembled in Dongguan, China

26 25 24 23 22   1 2 3 4 5

CONTENTS

INTRODUCTION

The *Jurassic Park* and *Jurassic World* trilogies have offered the world unforgettable films packed with screams, thrills, and adventures sixty-five million years in the making. On these pages, you'll find fifteen spectacular sticker puzzles featuring your favorite Jurassic characters and dinosaurs from the most iconic scenes from all six blockbuster films. With more than one hundred stickers per puzzle, you'll be challenged to the limit as you piece together images of moments you can never forget. You'll also find an exciting Jurassic Bite on each spread, offering fun facts or story details you might have missed.

INSTRUCTIONS

Each sticker puzzle features a framed outline. Within the outline are geometric spaces that offer hints as to where each sticker goes. You'll find the stickers starting on page 52. Apply each one to the corresponding shape in the outline and watch as the scene takes shape! The stickers can be reused in case you make a mistake. If you need a little help, solutions to the puzzles begin on page 36.

The pages in this book are perforated, so you can tear out the puzzles, stickers, and solutions to lay them out as you work. Solve the puzzles solo or as a group to tackle them together.

PUZZLES

WELCOME TO JURASSIC PARK

Paleontologist Dr. Alan Grant and Paleobotanist Dr. Ellie Sattler are unearthing a dinosaur skeleton when a helicopter arrives carrying industrialist John Hammond. The mogul has come to seek the expertise of these two world-renowned authorities on dinosaurs and their habitat.

John, founder of bioengineering start-up InGen Technologies, Inc.,

reveals that he has purchased an island, Isla Nublar, 120 miles west of Costa Rica and turned it into a "biological preserve." He just needs the scientists' stamp of approval to reassure investors his park is safe.

Drs. Grant and Sattler politely decline; their dig is not finished. But when John offers them enough money to fund three years of research, they can't refuse.

Aboard the helicopter heading to the island, the scientists meet John Hammond's lawyer Donald Gennaro and another expert: the offbeat, but brilliant, mathematician and chaos theorist Dr. Ian Malcolm. The helicopter races across the ocean, and then it soars high above majestic Isla Nublar to reveal a tropical paradise brimming with lush mountains, rainforests, and waterfalls.

John offers the group a warm welcome to his new enterprise, "Jurassic Park," an amusement park like nothing the world has ever seen. Drs. Grant and Sattler are awestruck as they behold what should be absolutely impossible—living, breathing dinosaurs!

At the park's Visitor Center and genetics laboratory, the group observes scientists extracting dinosaur DNA from mosquitos fossilized

in hardened tree sap, also called amber. A welcome video explains that millions of years ago the insects fed on dinosaur blood, and what is left still harbors enough of the creatures' DNA to allow scientists to clone new animals. John Hammond introduces his guests to Lead Genetic Biologist Dr. Henry Wu, who shows them the miracle of a dinosaur egg hatching.

But Dr. Malcolm is far more worried than impressed, warning that his hosts' cavalier attitude toward genetic manipulation is playing with fire. Dr. Malcolm's words hang in the air as Dr. Grant learns that the newborn dinosaur he is holding is a *Velociraptor*, one of the most cunning and fierce dinosaurs that ever lived.

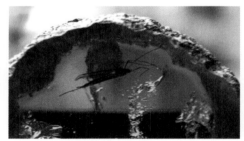

JURASSIC BITE

Although dinosaurs resemble reptiles, they share more similarities with present-day birds, according to Dr. Alan Grant. In fact, a radar image of a buried *Velociraptor* skeleton reveals it has bird-like characteristics, including a backward-facing pelvic bone and vertebrae full of air sacs and hollows.

"LIFE WILL NOT BE CONTAINED. LIFE BREAKS FREE. IT EXPANDS TO NEW TERRITORIES."
—DR. IAN MALCOLM

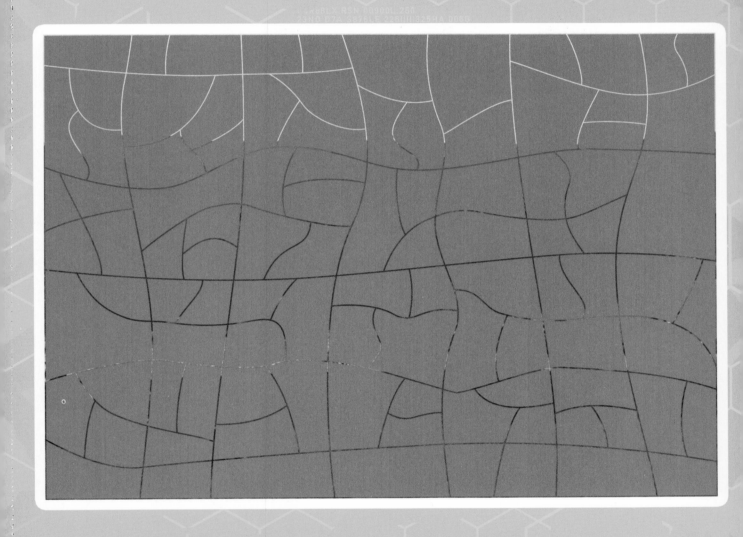

LIFE FINDS A WAY

The facility's disgruntled computer programmer, Dennis Nedry, has arrived at an off-island site to rendezvous with an employee of Biosyn, the biggest competitor of InGen. The liaison is prepared to pay a hefty bribe in exchange for Dennis' promise to steal Jurassic Park's precious fertilized dinosaur embryos.

scientists ponder the ethical and practical implications of cloning extinct prehistoric animals. Dr. Malcolm suggests his host's grand experiment was hastily conceived and will not end well.

Later, John Hammond's grandchildren, Lex and Tim, join the tour. Their grandfather is eager to see how the youngsters react to the attractions because, as he notes, they are Jurassic Park's "target audience." He sends everyone into the park then observes their journey from the control room. However, the industrialist's dry run hits some snags. First, the only dinosaur the group sees is a sick *Triceratops*. On top of that, they learn a tropical cyclone is headed straight for Isla Nublar. The park's managers call the visitors back, but Dr. Sattler insists on staying with a park veterinarian to figure out what has sickened the *Triceratops*.

The looming storm is also a huge problem for Dennis. Now he must act faster than planned to steal and deliver the embryos. Dennis informs

John that he is temporarily rebooting the park's security system while going for a quick snack. Instead, Dennis races to the embryo storage room to load frozen dinosaur embryos into a cooling container disguised as a shaving-cream can.

With the electric grid down due to the storm, the tour vehicles grind to a halt next to the *Tyrannosaurus rex*'s paddock. With the park's electric fences also disabled, the clever *T. rex* escapes!

Back in the park, John Hammond's guests visit a paddock, where a dinosaur devours a live cow behind high walls. The horrible sounds unnerve the group, but the business mogul takes it in stride, merely noting it might be time for their lunch too. In a private dining room, the

JURASSIC BITE

The *Triceratops* is about twenty-nine feet long and twelve feet tall, with specialized jaws packed with teeth that act as enormous scissors. The creatures can slice through any kind of plant but have a bad habit of eating West Indian lilac berries, which make them ill.

> "DINOSAURS AND MAN, TWO SPECIES SEPARATED BY SIXTY-FIVE MILLION YEARS OF EVOLUTION, HAVE JUST BEEN SUDDENLY THROWN BACK INTO THE MIX TOGETHER."
> —DR. ALAN GRANT

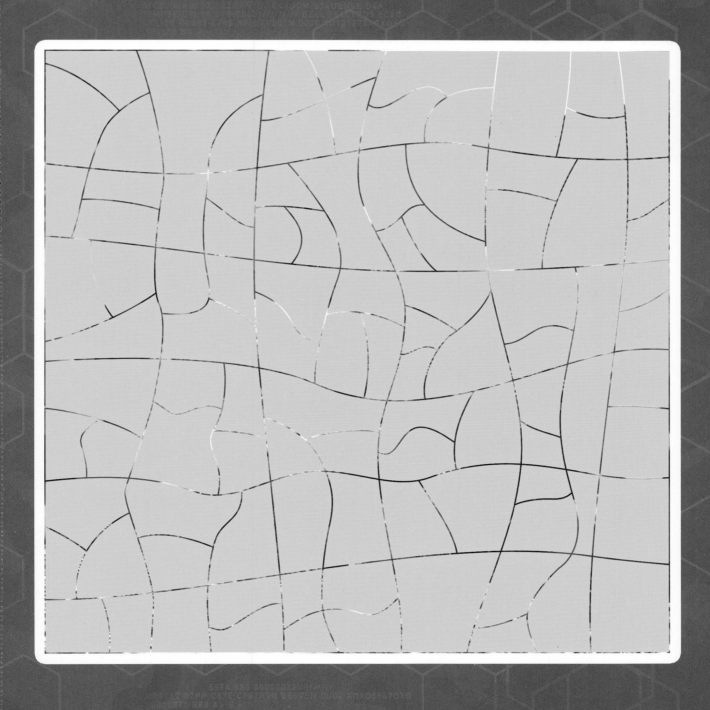

JURASSIC PARK

With the grid down, John Hammond's grandchildren remain stuck in their vehicle with park lawyer, Donald Gennaro. Suddenly, a severed goat leg splats onto the car, and the snarling *T. rex* is fast behind it. The terrified lawyer bolts out of the car to a bathroom, while Lex shines a flashlight outside. The beam attracts the dinosaur, and it flips the car with the children in it. Dr. Grant and Dr. Malcolm lure the creature away, but it smashes into the latrine, and the lawyer meets his demise. Dr. Grant saves the kids in a daring rescue.

Meanwhile, John, Dr. Sattler, and Jurassic Park Chief Engineer Ray Arnold

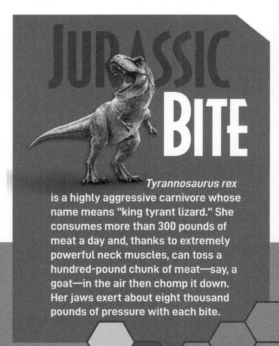

try to guess Dennis Nedry's computer password so they can get the park back online. But it's no use, and Dennis is already racing across the island with the stolen dinosaur embryos...until he's cornered by a *Dilophosaurus* that does away with him.

Game warden Robert Muldoon and Dr. Sattler search for the children only to find an injured Dr. Malcolm and a *T. rex* out for blood. Dr. Grant and the kids are already traversing the island. At dusk, they seek shelter in a tree and meet a friendly *Brachiosaurus*. Dr. Grant spots hatched dinosaur eggs and realizes the creatures—all female—have reproduced. He surmises some switched gender because they were engineered with DNA from West African frogs, amphibians known to adapt in a same-sex environment.

John sends the engineer to the maintenance shed to reboot the park system. Ray never returns, so Dr. Sattler searches for him, only to discover a raging raptor

has taken his life! Outside, more raptors attack the game warden. Dr. Grant, Lex, and Tim finally arrive at the visitor center. But when Dr. Grant momentarily leaves the children, *Velociraptors* terrorize them in the kitchen. The kids escape to the control room, where they meet up with Drs. Grant and Sattler. Lex, who has a way with computers, gets the park back online. Everyone reunites only to be cornered by raptors. All seems lost until the *T. rex* battles the smaller dinosaurs, allowing the exhausted, battered humans to escape outside and onto a waiting helicopter.

JURASSIC BITE

Tyrannosaurus rex is a highly aggressive carnivore whose name means "king tyrant lizard." She consumes more than 300 pounds of meat a day and, thanks to extremely powerful neck muscles, can toss a hundred-pound chunk of meat—say, a goat—in the air then chomp it down. Her jaws exert about eight thousand pounds of pressure with each bite.

> "YOUR SCIENTISTS WERE SO PREOCCUPIED WITH WHETHER OR NOT THEY COULD, THEY DIDN'T STOP TO THINK IF THEY SHOULD."
> —DR. IAN MALCOLM

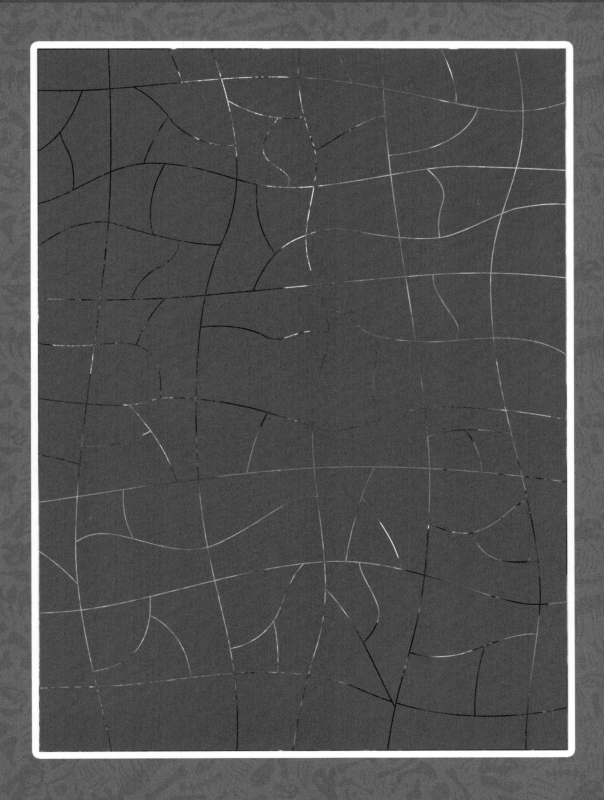

ALL NEW MISTAKES

Four years after the debacle at Jurassic Park, an ailing John Hammond is a changed man who is far less interested in turning a profit than protecting the genetically engineered dinosaurs he helped create. The animals now roam free on a second island, Isla Sorna, located eighty-seven miles southwest of Isla Nublar. It is also

known as "Site B," the place where the dinosaurs were bred.

But when a wealthy family leaves their yacht to have lunch on the deserted island, their daughter is attacked by dozens of tiny *Compsognathus*. The child survives, but the frightening encounter is a harbinger

of things to come. Meanwhile, John's nephew, Peter Ludlow, has used the attack as an excuse to wrest control of the financially strapped InGen from his uncle. John fears for the dinosaurs' future, so he asks mathematician and chaos theorist Dr. Ian Malcolm to lead an expedition that will visually document the dinosaurs in their habitat, with the hope to garner public support for protecting the animals from exploitation. Dr. Malcolm has no interest in repeating his Jurassic Park nightmare, nor is he thrilled that InGen has sullied his reputation by publically dismissing his horror stories as fantasy. John convinces Dr. Malcolm to take the job by revealing that Malcolm's girlfriend, Paleontologist Dr. Sarah Harding, is part of his team and already on the island.

Dr. Malcolm flies to Isla Sorna along with equipment specialist Eddie Carr and documentarian Nick Van Owen. The trio locates a

happy Dr. Harding photographing a herd of *Stegosaurus*. Dr. Malcolm, on the other hand, is quite unhappy to discover that his teenage daughter, Kelly, has stowed away in an InGen trailer and that Peter Ludlow has come with mercenaries and big-game hunters to ship the dinosaurs to populate a new iteration of Jurassic Park in San Diego. Head game hunter, Roland Tembo, has agreed to lead his team on one condition—that he can hunt and kill a male *Tyrannosaurus rex*.

JURASSIC BITE

Compsognathus, or "Compys" as paleontologists call them, are tiny dinosaurs that weigh only about two pounds and make chirping sounds. The animals are mostly solitary but will congregate for easy feeding. For example, they'll nibble on a carcass that a larger dinosaur has left behind.

> **"TAKING DINOSAURS OFF THIS ISLAND IS THE WORST IDEA IN THE LONG, SAD HISTORY OF BAD IDEAS."**
> —DR. IAN MALCOLM

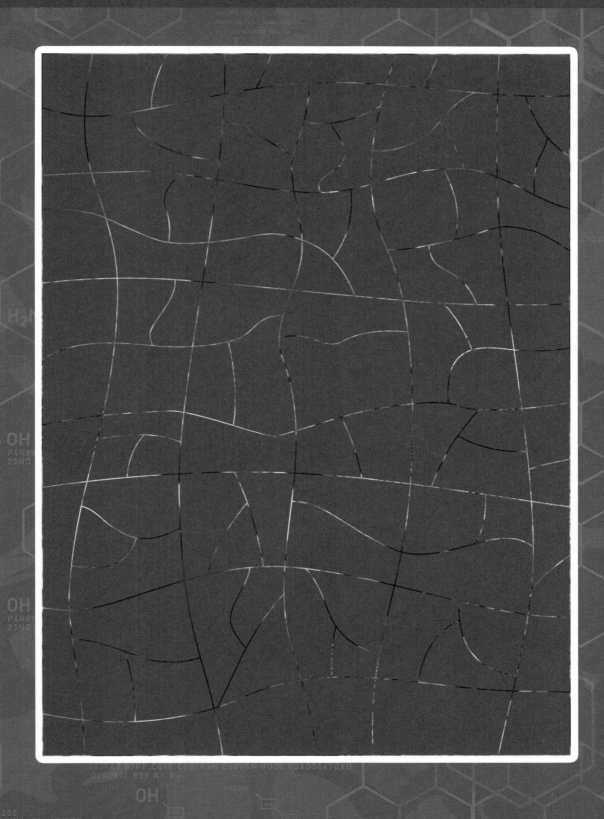

FOLLOW THE SCREAMS

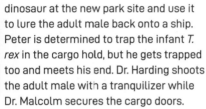

Dr. Sarah Harding and documentarian Nick Van Owen release the dinosaurs captured by the InGen team, but the animals rampage

through the company's base camp. Nick rescues a wailing baby *T. rex* that Roland Tembo has chained up to lure the adult male. Nick and Dr. Harding bring the infant dinosaur into an abandoned trailer, where they treat it for a broken leg. When the adult dinosaurs arrive, Dr. Harding and Nick carefully release the baby dinosaur, but the outraged parents decimate the trailer. Eddie Carr valiantly saves his

colleagues but loses his life in the process.

Peter Ludlow's team finally rescues Dr. Malcolm, Dr. Harding, Nick, and Kelly, but both groups' communications systems are out, so they must work together to find an old InGen base to reach the outside world. Roland's hunting cohort gets separated from the group and is killed by the tiny but fierce *Compys*. Later, *Tyrannosaurus rexes* launch a deadly attack on the campsite, and when the InGen workers flee, *Velociraptors* attack again.

At last, Dr. Malcolm gets everyone to the base and summons a helicopter. As they depart the island, they can see that Peter's team has captured and sedated the adult male *T. rex*. Then more workers arrive to ship the dinosaurs to San Diego on the *SS Venture*.

But things do not go as planned. When the ship arrives in the U.S., it crashes into the pier, and the *T. rex* rampages through the city streets. Dr. Malcolm and Dr. Harding find the baby

dinosaur at the new park site and use it to lure the adult male back onto a ship. Peter is determined to trap the infant *T. rex* in the cargo hold, but he gets trapped too and meets his end. Dr. Harding shoots the adult male with a tranquilizer while Dr. Malcolm secures the cargo doors.

In the end, the adult and baby *Tyrannosaurus rexes* return safely to Isla Sorna. John Hammond announces that the United States and Costa Rica have declared the island a nature preserve.

JURASSIC BITE

Paleontologist Dr. Sarah Harding and documentarian Nick Van Owen rescue an injured baby *T. rex* that is less than two weeks old. Dr. Harding warns that if she does not treat the infant's fractured leg quickly, he'll get picked off by predators. So she sets and wraps the limb and administers an antibiotic. Moments later, the baby dinosaur's angry parents arrive, proving Dr. Harding's theory that adult *T. rexes* definitely have parental instincts.

> "SOMEWHERE ON THIS ISLAND IS THE GREATEST PREDATOR THAT EVER LIVED. THE SECOND GREATEST PREDATOR MUST TAKE HIM DOWN."
> —ROLAND TEMBO

FOLLOW THE SCREAMS / Stickers on page 61. Solution on page 41.

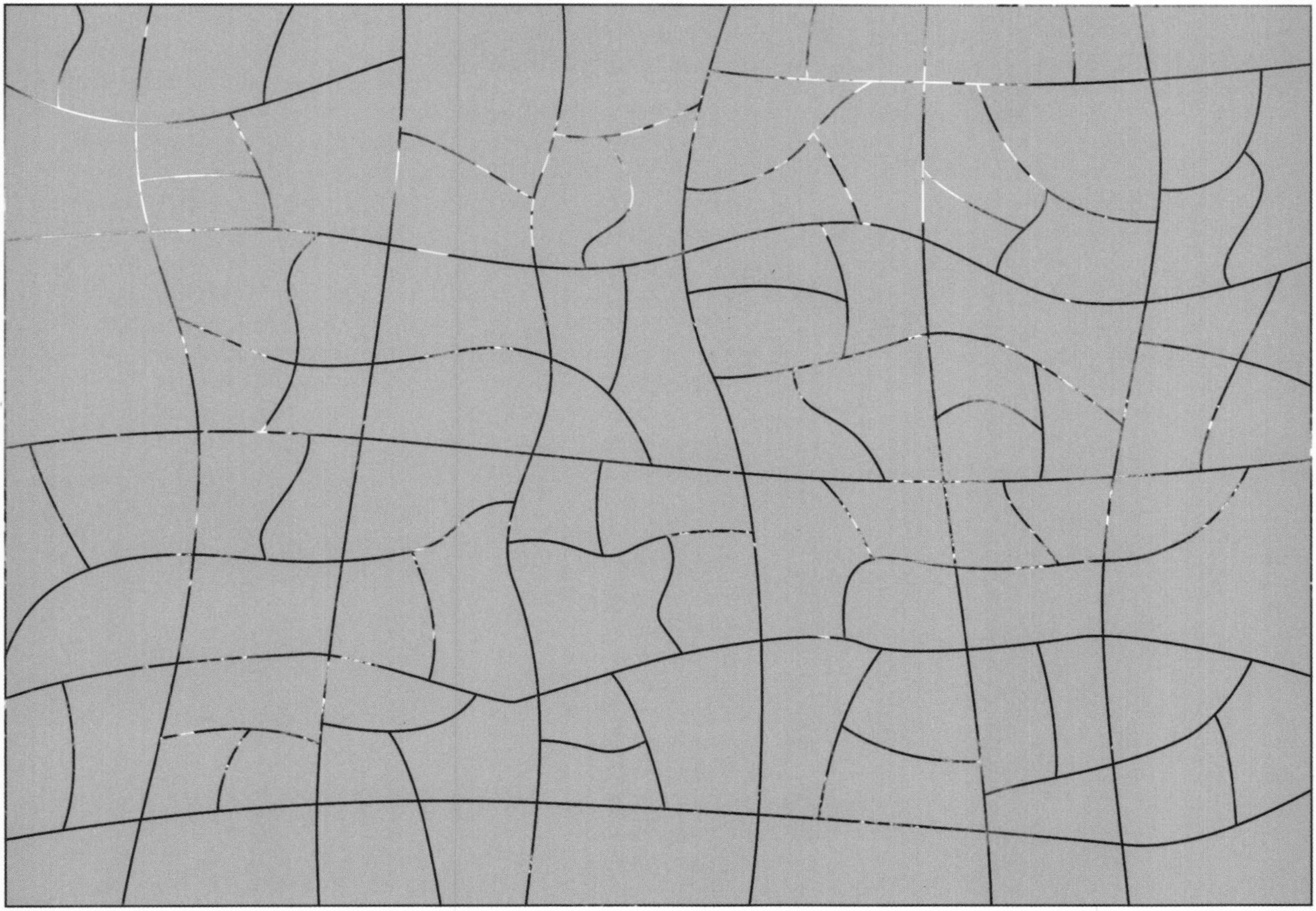

SITE B

A wealthy couple, Paul and Amanda Kirby, offer to fund Dr. Alan Grant's research if he'll guide them on an aerial tour of Isla Sorna. But Dr. Grant refuses... until Paul offers him a blank check. The paleontologist's only stipulation is that his young colleague Billy Brennan comes along. Billy had impressed Dr. Grant by using a 3-D printer to replicate

a *Velociraptor* larynx that can mimic the animals' calls.

As the plane approaches Isla Sorna, Dr. Grant is appalled to learn the Kirbys have no intention of keeping the plane airborne. The moment the group steps onto the landing strip, a *Spinosaurus* goes after a mercenary that the couple hired for protection. The pilot tries to taxi away from the danger, but as the soldier waves to stop their departure, the dinosaur launches a deadly attack on him. The animal hits the aircraft, causing it to crash into the dense jungle. The *Spinosaurus* demolishes the plane before eating another mercenary—the one with the group's satellite phone!

The survivors escape one dinosaur, only to encounter another: a raging *T. rex*. Fortunately, the animals fight each other instead of the humans, who manage to escape. As the group journeys on, Dr. Grant discovers that the Kirbys are not who they say they are: they've really come to Isla Sorna to rescue their twelve-year-old son, Eric, who, along with a family friend, crashed on the island in a parasailing accident eight weeks prior. Paul and Amanda reveal they are divorced and that the "friend" is Amanda's boyfriend. But the distraught parents insist they need the paleontologist's help navigating the restricted island. Dr. Grant is quick to inform them he's never set foot on Isla Sorna, also known as Site B. He's only been on Isla Nublar.

As the search for Eric continues, the group discovers that Amanda's boyfriend didn't survive the parasailing accident. Billy Brennan collects his nylon sail in case they need it in an emergency. Dr. Grant is separated from his team, but Eric, who has survived on food and water from an abandoned supply truck, rescues him and he reunites with his overjoyed parents.

JURASSIC BITE

The semi-aquatic *Spinosaurus* hunts a lot like a grizzly bear, wading into water to catch slippery fish with its claws. The massive dinosaur's extra-dense bones help it achieve neutral buoyancy while swimming.

> **"NO FORCE ON EARTH OR HEAVEN COULD GET ME ON THAT ISLAND."**
> —DR. ALAN GRANT

THE BEST INTENTIONS

JURASSIC PARK III

Moments after the Kirbys reunite with their son Eric, the *Spinosaurus* attacks again. The group heads into an abandoned observatory, where Dr. Grant discovers that his colleague, Billy Brennan, has stolen two raptor eggs. The young paleontologist tells his mentor he'd intended to sell the eggs to fund a dig site. Dr. Grant is uninterested in his excuses. Besides, he has other plans for the eggs. He'll hold on to them for safe passage—the raptors won't harm the humans as long as they have their offspring.

Next, the group wanders into a *Pteranodon* aviary. One of the flying creatures takes off with Eric, and, in a moment of sacrifice, Billy dons the parasail and rescues him. Everyone is certain Billy has been killed in the process.

Dr. Grant and the Kirbys spot a boat, but before they board, they hear the satellite phone ringing in a pile of dinosaur droppings. They try calling for help, but the *Spinosaurus* attacks again, puncturing the boat's gas tank and submerging the craft. It looks as if Dr. Grant and the others are doomed until they get ahold of Dr. Ellie Sattler for a few moments and she hears their cries for help. They escape the sinking vessel, and Paul climbs the rigging to distract the dinosaur. At the same time, Dr. Grant shoots a flare into the river to light the gasoline on fire and scare the animal off.

The next day, the survivors head for the shore but are surrounded by snarling raptors. Dr. Grant knows the animals won't attack as long as they have the eggs. To get the group to safety, he blows through Billy's fabricated raptor larynx as a distraction. They gently lay down the dinosaur eggs, and the confused raptors run off with their unhatched offspring.

Finally, Dr. Grant and the Kirbys spot Marines and Navy personnel arriving on the coast and find Billy aboard one of their choppers. He's injured but alive. The Kirbys are relieved to have survived the ordeal and grateful for one another. It looks as if they might become a happy family once again.

JURASSIC BITE

Pteranodon means "toothless wing," an apt description for these fierce, flying reptiles with crested heads, long bills, and wingspans of up to twenty feet. They originally lived seventy-five million years ago and survived by hunting fish. They are one of many flying species belonging to the *Pterosaur* genus.

"SOME OF THE WORST THINGS IMAGINABLE HAVE BEEN DONE WITH THE BEST INTENTIONS."
—DR. ALAN GRANT

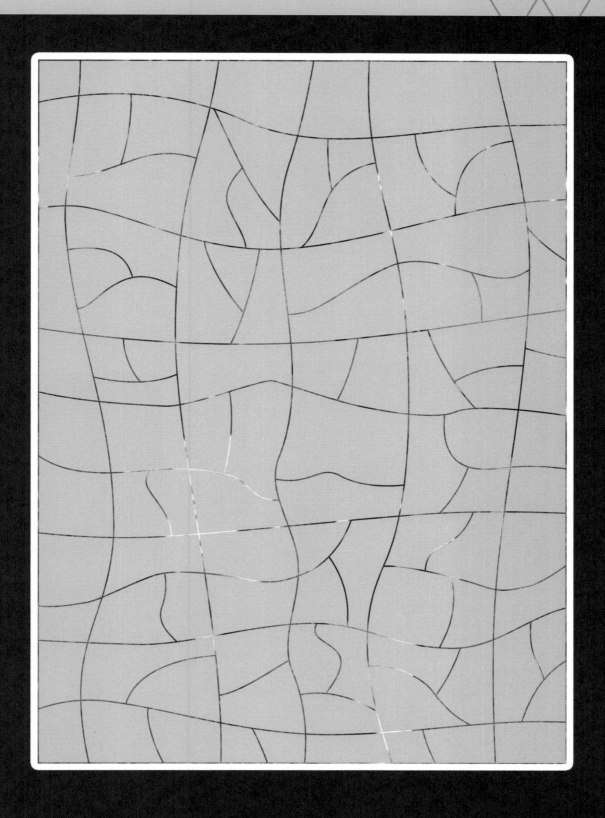

JURASSIC WORLD

A new theme park, Jurassic World, has risen on Isla Nublar. The thriving enterprise is run by Operations Manager Claire Dearing, a serious businesswoman with little time for anything but work—not even her visiting nephews, Gray and Zach Mitchell. The boys are eager to tour the park with their aunt, whom they haven't seen in seven years. But instead, Claire sends her assistant to be the boys' guide so she can focus on corporate sponsors ready to tour the park's genetics laboratory. She tells them the public has grown too used to dinosaurs. As Claire says, people want them bigger, louder, and with more teeth. She promises to deliver just that with the park's newest asset, the Indominus rex, the world's first genetically modified hybrid dinosaur. InGen Lead Genetic Biologist Dr. Henry Wu arrives to explain how his creation is a miracle of modern science.

Jurassic World was built by Masrani Global Corporation, founded by the adventurous, helicopter-flying Simon Masrani. He acquired InGen and its dinosaur assets from John Hammond and is determined to honor the man's dying wish to "spare no expense" and ensure visitors have fun and that the dinosaurs are happy.

Masrani is awed when he meets the Indominus rex for the first time but worries the paddock is not strong enough. So he asks Claire to call in

Owen Grady, a former Navy officer and animal behaviorist at the park, who is there to conduct research on *Velociraptors*—dangerous dinosaurs known to be escape artists.

Owen is training four raptors that he's named Blue, Echo, Delta, and Charlie. The animals respond eagerly to Owen's commands, and it is clear they have bonded with him. But InGen Head of Security Vic Hoskins has his eyes on the animals for his own purposes. He believes there is a fortune to be made training the raptors as military weapons.

JURASSIC BITE

InGen Head of Security Vic Hoskins believes the ultra-intelligent *Velociraptors* (whose name means "swift thief") will make excellent military weapons because they can work together to take down prey much larger than themselves. What's most important, though, is that the dinosaurs can bond with human beings, making them highly trainable.

> **"THE INDOMINUS WASN'T BRED. SHE WAS DESIGNED. SHE WILL BE FIFTY FEET LONG WHEN FULLY GROWN. BIGGER THAN THE *T. REX*."**
> —DR. HENRY WU

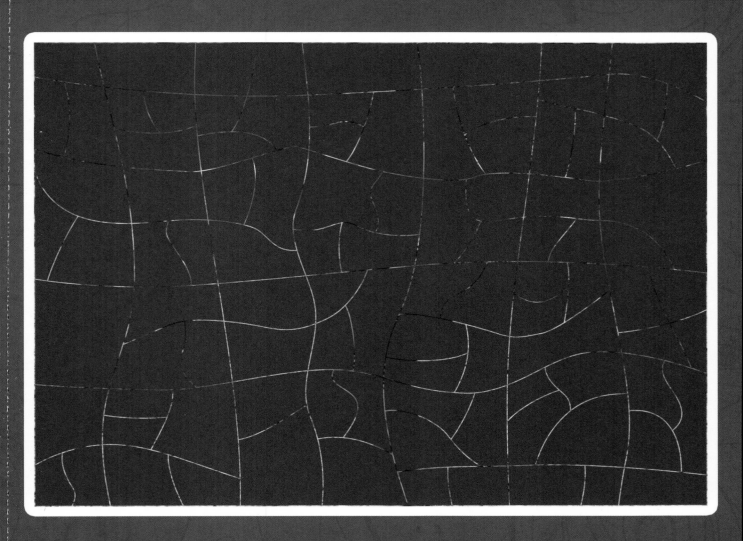

EVERYONE REMAIN CALM

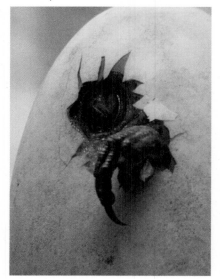

Claire Dearing's nephews, Zach and Gray, ditch their guide and take off to enjoy the park on their own. Elsewhere on the island, Owen Grady arrives to assess the Indominus' paddock but is alarmed to find out the animal has been bred in captivity without contact with other creatures. Suddenly, the park's heat sensors indicate the dinosaur has escaped! Claire puts out an alert and takes off for the control room while Owen and two workers enter the paddock. But the creature has somehow evaded the heat sensors and is still inside!

The Indominus charges Owen and the workers, who escape just as the paddock door closes. But not fast enough. The dinosaur bursts through and devours the two workers. Owen manages to survive, but the deadly creature is now roaming the island. Claire assures her team the animal will receive a shock if it goes near a perimeter fence, while Masrani forbids issuing a park-wide alert. He insists Jurassic World's Asset Containment Unit (ACU) can handle any escaped animal. But he's wrong; the Indominus rex lays waste to most of the unit's men.

Owen recognizes that the hybrid dinosaur is ultra-intelligent and cunning, so he insists they close the park and destroy the animal. But Claire is only willing to evacuate visitors from the resort's north sector. Unfortunately, it's where her nephews have just stepped into a Gyrosphere and are headed for a restricted area.

Masrani and Dr. Wu realize the Indominus can camouflage itself and hide from thermal technology because the animal was created using the DNA from cuttlefish and tree frogs, which have those properties.

Meanwhile, Zach and Gray face off with the massive Indominus, which cracks their Gyrosphere like a walnut. The boys escape by jumping over a waterfall. Claire and Owen frantically search for the boys as chaos ensues in the park.

JURASSIC BITE

Jurassic World's glass-enclosed Gyropsheres seem to defy gravity. Their secret is ball bearings that that keep the vehicle upright no matter how rough the terrain. These gyro-rolling vehicles are operated with a joystick and glide at 5 m.p.h. past some of park's most docile dinosaurs—*Apatosaurus*, *Stegosaurus*, *Parasaurolophus*, and *Triceratops*.

> "SHE DOES NOT EVEN KNOW WHAT SHE IS...
> SHE WILL KILL EVERYTHING THAT MOVES."
> —OWEN GRADY

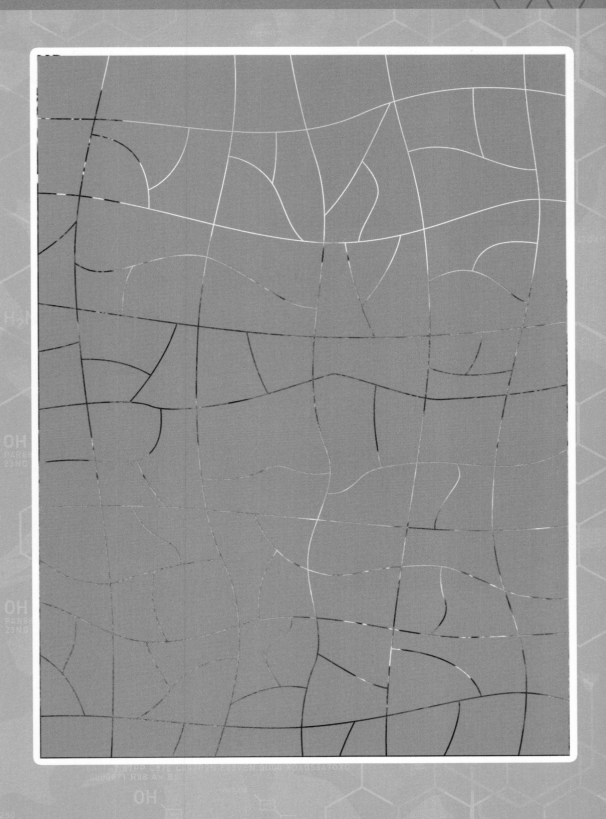

THE NEW ALPHA

As the control room techs track the Indominus rex, InGen Head of Security Vic Hoskins sees an opportunity to test his theories. He wants Simon Masrani to use Owen Grady's *Velociraptors* to hunt the rampaging animal. But Simon refuses.

Meanwhile, Zach and Gray stumble upon the abandoned ruins of the

original Jurassic Park, where they start an old vehicle and drive it back to the Innovation Center. Claire and Owen run from the raging Indominus rex, while Simon flies himself and members of the Asset Containment Unit in a helicopter to hunt it down. The gargantuan animal smashes into the park's aviary, releasing a flock of *Pteranodons* that crash the helicopter, killing everyone aboard, including Simon. Next, the creatures

head for the resort, where they terrorize a capacity crowd. Gray and Zach finally reunite with their aunt and Owen.

With Simon gone, Vic calls on InGen's armed tactical force to take over the park—he is ready to sic the *Velociraptors* on the Indominus. Owen hates the idea but has no choice but to cooperate. The four *Velociraptors* find the rampaging dinosaur, but to everyone's shock, it appears they can communicate with it! It's discovered that the giant animal has been engineered using *Velociraptor* DNA and is now the pack's alpha. One of Owen's raptors is killed during an attack on the InGen soldiers. Dr. Wu gets off the island with dinosaur embryos, and Owen, Claire, and the boys find Vic grabbing whatever is left in the lab— but the *Velociraptors* take him out too.

In the mayhem, Owen and Claire work together to save lives. Owen uses his bond with the raptors to get them to fend off the Indominus. But it's no match. So Claire

releases the *Tyrannosaurus rex*, and a battle ensues between the two deadly giants. Even the *T. rex* cannot win until the remaining *Velociraptor*, Blue, joins in to lure the Indominus to the lagoon, where she's pulled underwater by the massive *Mosasaurus*.

All the survivors are evacuated, and Zach and Gray are reunited with their parents. Owen and Claire survived the unthinkable together.

JURASSIC BITE

Simon Masrani is a novice helicopter pilot just two days away from getting his license. So it is no surprise that he fails to outmaneuver a flock of *Pteranodons* released when the Indominus rex crashed through Jurassic World's 430,000-square-foot aviary. The domed structure is home to two species of *Pterosaur*: *Pteranodon* and *Dimorphodon*.

> **"I'VE BEEN WORKING FOR TWO YEARS ON APPLICATIONS FOR THOSE RAPTORS. THEY CAN HUNT AND KILL THAT CREATURE."**
> **—VIC HOSKINS**

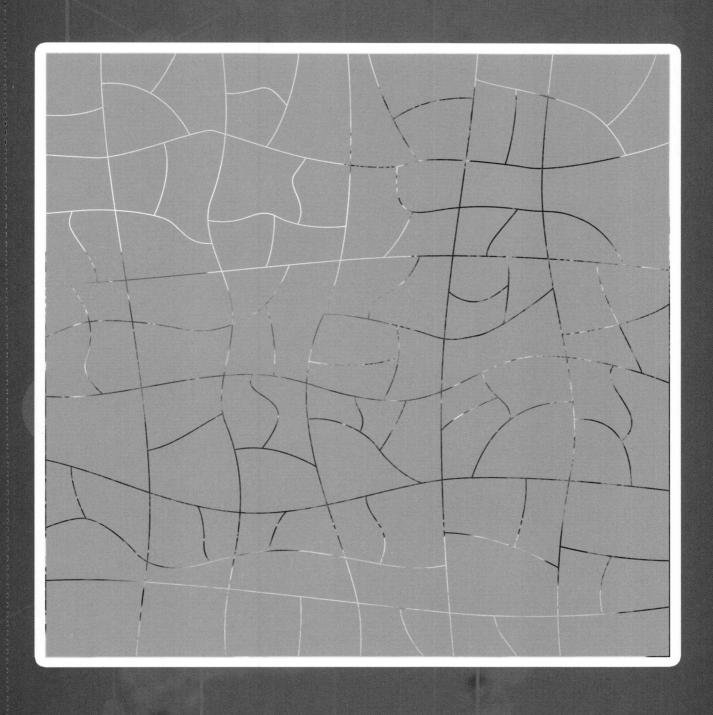

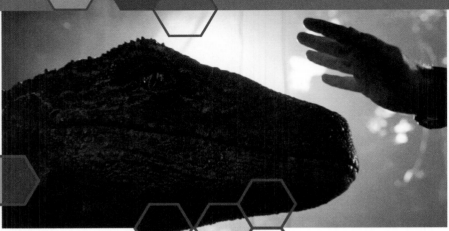

T hree years after the Indominus rex tore through Jurassic World, mercenaries collect DNA from the hybrid dinosaur's carcass lying at the bottom of the Mosasaurus Lagoon. What they don't realize is the massive aquatic *Mosasaurus* is still alive! It devours their small submarine, and then a *T. rex* attacks on land. The humans escape in a chopper and fly off with the Indominus rex's genetic material.

Meanwhile, Dr. Ian Malcolm dissuades a U.S. Senate committee from rescuing the dinosaurs from an active volcano because, he says, it's wrong to interfere with nature. Jurassic World's former operations manager, Claire Dearing, now an animal advocate, watches the proceedings from her Dinosaur Protection Group offices and is appalled.

After the hearing, John Hammond's former business partner, Sir Benjamin Lockwood, summons Claire to his Northern California estate to ask for her help relocating the endangered dinosaurs to a new island sanctuary. His right-hand man, Eli Mills, explains that only her handprint can reactivate Jurassic World's dinosaur tracking system, and they also need her help navigating the abandoned park. Sir Benjamin is mostly focused on saving the last living *Velociraptor*, Blue, considered one of the most intelligent creatures on the planet. Claire agrees to the mission and calls on her former colleague Owen Grady to help, since he raised the raptor.

Claire and Owen, along with systems analyst Franklin Webb and paleo-veterinarian Zia Rodriguez, fly to Isla Nublar and meet a mercenary team commanded by Ken Wheatley. Franklin locates Blue through an implanted tracking device, but when Owen starts to regain her trust, the commander shoots her. An outraged Owen goes for Ken but gets tranquilized.

Lava consumes the island, and dinosaurs stampede down the mountain. Claire, Franklin, and Owen make a harrowing escape only to find the commander loading animals—including wounded Blue—onto a cargo ship about to leave. The three realize they've been tricked and sneak aboard, where they reunite with Zia, who is being forced to treat Blue. The group helps save Blue's life with a blood transfusion from a tranquilized *T. rex.*

JURASSIC BITE

The genetic sample from the Indominus rex carcass will reveal that Dr. Henry Wu's hybrid dinosaur was a marvel of genetic engineering created by combining DNA from the *T. rex*, *Velociraptor*, *Carnotaurus*, *Gigantosaurus*, *Rugops*, *Majungasaurus*, and *Therizinosaurus* with that of modern animals like viper snakes, tree frogs, and cuttlefish.

> "THESE CREATURES DON'T NEED OUR PROTECTION. THEY NEED OUR ABSENCE."
> —SIR BENJAMIN LOCKWOOD

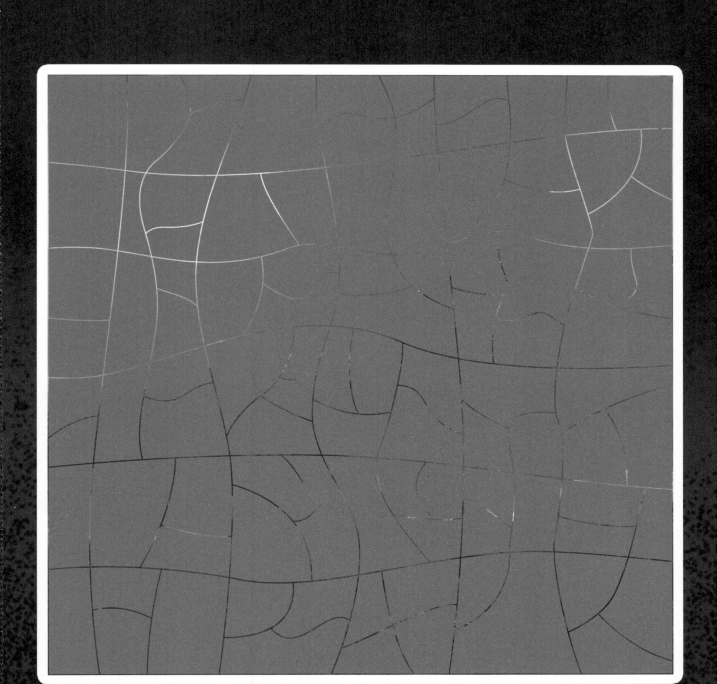

FORCED TO COEXIST

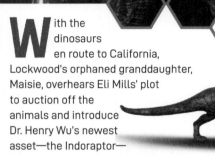

With the dinosaurs en route to California, Lockwood's orphaned granddaughter, Maisie, overhears Eli Mills' plot to auction off the animals and introduce Dr. Henry Wu's newest asset—the Indoraptor— a "weaponized" animal created with a combination of DNA from the Indominus rex and a *Velociraptor*. Now Dr. Wu wants Blue's DNA so he can develop an Indoraptor that can respond to human commands. Maisie tells her grandfather about the plan, but soon Eli murders his elderly employer to keep the auction in motion. He also shakes Maisie's world by telling her she is a clone of the woman she thought was her mother.

Eli discovers Claire Dearing and Owen Grady on the property and locks them in a dinosaur cage so he can greet his guests. Owen, thinking fast, provokes a *Stygimoloch* into busting down the cell wall. On the auction floor, as dinosaurs are being shipped off to buyers' homes, Eli starts seeking bids for the Indoraptor. Dr. Wu objects, warning that the creature is only a prototype and too dangerous to sell. Owen releases the *Stygimoloch* into the auction room interrupting the bidding. As everyone runs out, Ken Wheatley tranquilizes the Indoraptor to extract one of its teeth for his trophy collection. He is then mauled to death, leaving the dinosaur to roam the estate, chasing Owen, Claire, and Maisie. Zia frees Blue, who saves the day by battling the Indoraptor to its death.

Claire realizes the estate's genetic laboratory has sprung a hydrogen cyanide gas leak, endangering the dinosaurs' lives. But she can't bring herself to set them loose on an unsuspecting world. Maisie, however, identifies with the genetically engineered creatures and frees them. The *T. rex* devours Eli and stomps on the Indominus rex bone he is trying to steal. The group escapes, and, in a tender moment, Owen bids farewell to Blue.

In the end, Dr. Malcolm addresses the U.S. Senate once again, warning that human beings needing to play God with genetics has brought a new, unpredictable age upon the earth, one in which dinosaurs and humans are now forced to coexist.

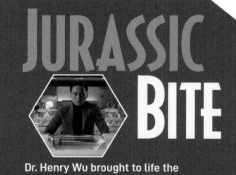

JURASSIC BITE

Dr. Henry Wu brought to life the hyper-intelligent *Velociraptors*, dinosaurs with the ability to communicate, plan, and bond with humans. Their intelligence is often compared to that of dolphins or whales, but Eli Mills asserts they are the second smartest animals on the planet, with humans ostensibly being the first.

> "WE'RE GONNA HAVE TO ADJUST TO NEW THREATS WE CAN'T IMAGINE. WE'VE ENTERED A NEW ERA."
> —DR. IAN MALCOLM

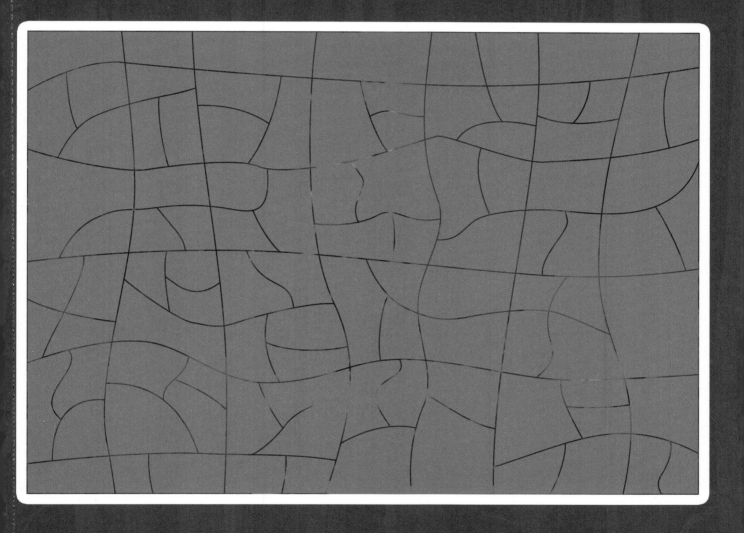

After years of adapting to strange new environments, dinosaurs of all species are living and thriving all around our world. No longer in the tropical jungles of Isla Nublar, clever Blue has learned to navigate the new world—and its far greater dangers—in the snowy Sierra Nevada Mountains, not far from Owen's cabin where he lives with Claire and Maisie. Blue's taken shelter in an abandoned school bus deep in the woods. A cracked egg from where her identical clone, Beta, hatched remains in a nest there.

Owen senses that blue is out there somewhere and is especially worried because it's now hunting season. But it's Blue who teaches Beta to hunt wolves and rabbits. When two gun-toting hunters spot the raptors and plan to take them down, Blue pounces, eliminating the threat.

Later near the cabin, Beta spies Maisie and stealthily approaches her. Maisie offers her food. Owen cautiously approaches them as he spies Blue, protective, behind Beta. Maisie follows Owen's lead and, suddenly, Blue snatches a dead fox and runs back to the woods with Beta. Owen tells Maisie to go inside while he follows the raptors, which she is not happy about. Later, she sneaks out on her bike.

While searching for Blue and Beta, Owen hears a loud screech coming from deep in the forest. As he runs toward

Blue's familiar sound, he sees the reason for her cries—dinosaur poachers are speeding off in a truck and have captured not only Beta but Maisie too! Owen quickly runs back to the cabin to get Claire. They have to move fast to try to save Maisie. As they head out, Blue appears. She approaches and scratches Owen's open palm—a warning? Owen promises Blue he will bring Beta back too.

JURASSIC BITE

Juvenile raptor Beta weighs just 55 pounds and has a lot of growing to do to reach her full size of around 500 pounds like her adult counterpart Blue, who can bite with a force of more than 8,000 Newtons—equivalent to a large American alligator.

"THE RAPTOR'S GOT A JUVENILE. IF YOU WANT IT, IT WON'T COME CHEAP."
—RAINN DELACOURT

STOP TRADE OF DINOSAURS

In an underground street market in Malta, where dinosaurs are illegally traded, Claire and Owen meet a cargo pilot named Kayla who agrees to fly them to Biosyn Genetics to find Maisie and Beta. As Kayla's plane approaches the massive valley compound situated in the Dolomite Mountains, a giant flying *Quetzalcoatlus* pursues the plane. The winged dinosaur latches onto one of the engines, crushing it and tearing it from the fuselage. As the plane rapidly descends, Owen ejects Claire's seat in an attempt to save her, as he goes down with Kayla inside the aircraft.

The plane crash lands on an icy dam not too far from Biosyn Genetics. Banged and bruised, Owen and Kayla survive, but they must tread lightly on the ice as they make their way toward the shore or risk cracking it, falling in, and freezing. On top of that, a huge, feathered *Pyroraptor* has appeared on the bank and is now watching them.

The stealthy *Pyroraptor* surprises them by swimming under the ice toward them. It eyes them through the frozen surface and waits. Suddenly, the ice cracks and Owen falls in. The ferocious dinosaur begins its pursuit. Luckily, Kayla is there to help Owen and pulls him out of the water just in time. But their troubles aren't over, as they must still find a way to get Maisie and Beta inside the seemingly impenetrable compound. More impending, they don't know where Claire landed and if she survived.

DINOSAUR SPOTTED HERE

JURASSIC BITE

The *Pyroraptor*, whose name means "fire thief," is a feathered dinosaur with enlarged curved claws on the second toe of each foot. Its stealth movements enable it to hunt its target even from underneath the icy waters of a frozen lake, as it waits for its victims to fall through the cracking ice above.

> "FUELED BY NEW ACCESS TO CLONING TECHNOLOGY AND CONTRABAND DNA, A GLOBAL BLACK MARKET HAS RISEN."
> —GEMMA ZHAO, JOURNALIST

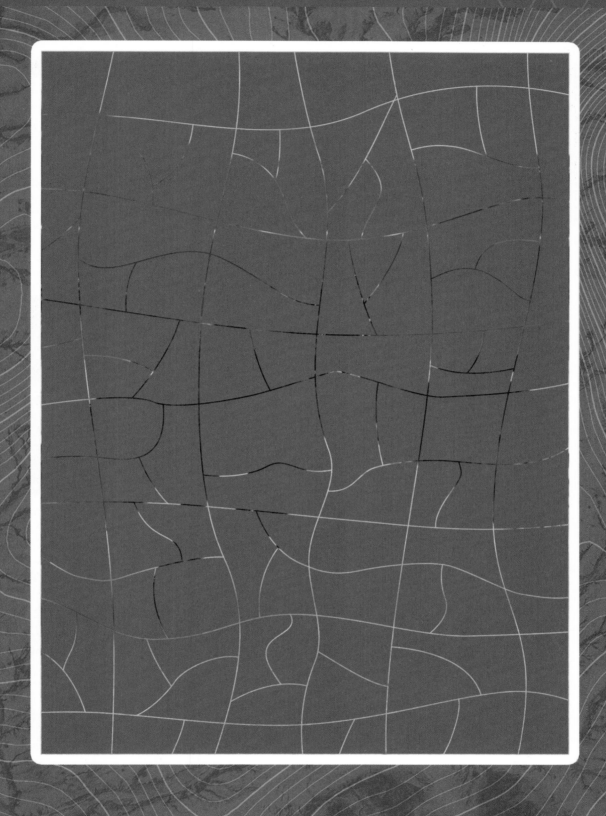

JURASSIC WORLD
DOMINION

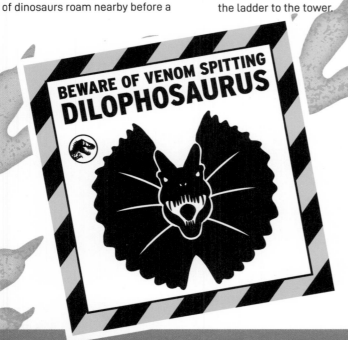

Separated from Owen and Kayla, Claire has a crash-landing of her own—right into a treetop in the forest of Biosyn Valley. But she is alive and, believing Owen and Kayla have surely perished in the plane, must navigate her own way to find Maisie. After wrestling with her seatbelt and parachute, Claire manages to slip out of the chair and safely down to the ground below. But danger is ever-present because, in this new world, there are dinosaurs lurking around every turn.

She hides in some brush as a couple of dinosaurs roam nearby before a *T. rex* and *Giganotosaurus* jockey for food. When the coast is clear, Claire rushes toward an elevated outpost. The metal ladder for Claire to climb into the safety of the Outpost Tower above can't come down fast enough, as a *Dilophosaurus* appears and follows her. She is trapped on the valley floor facing the dangerous dinosaur and it attacks! It emits its highly toxic spit, but Kayla catches it in her leather-gloved hand and saves Claire. Thrilled to find each other alive, the trio staves off the dinosaur together and races up the ladder to the tower.

From this vantage point, they see a way into Biosyn Genetics and begin making their way to rescue Maisie and Beta—but not before chaos befalls them and the entire Biosyn Genetics compound. Can humans and dinosaurs truly coexist?

DO NOT WALK RUN!

BEWARE OF VENOM SPITTING DILOPHOSAURUS

JURASSIC BITE

Weighing in at 900 pounds, *Dilophosaurus* is an aggressive carnivore that ambushes its victims. It chatters like an owl and has twin crests on either side of the skull that serve as display signals to show off to other members of the species.

"LET'S FINISH THIS."
—DR. ELLIE SATTLER

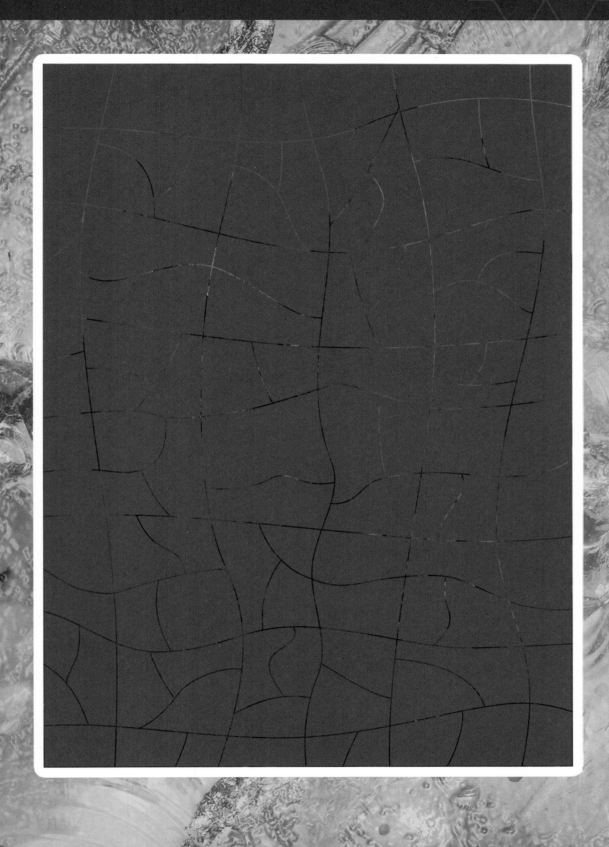

SOLUTIONS

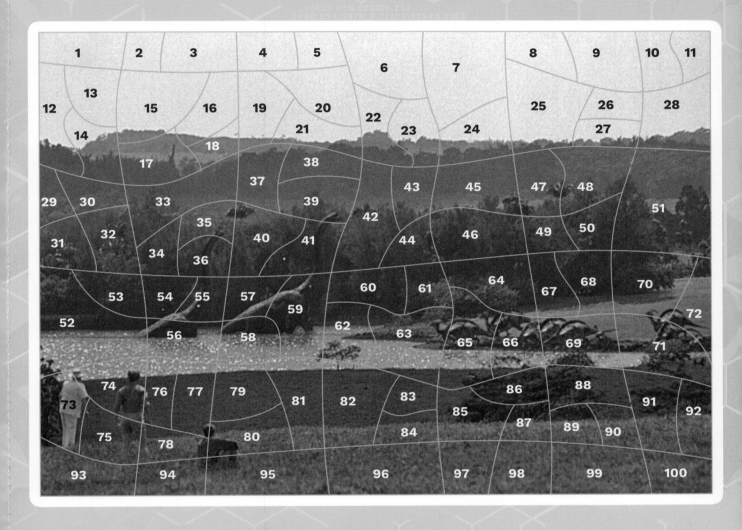

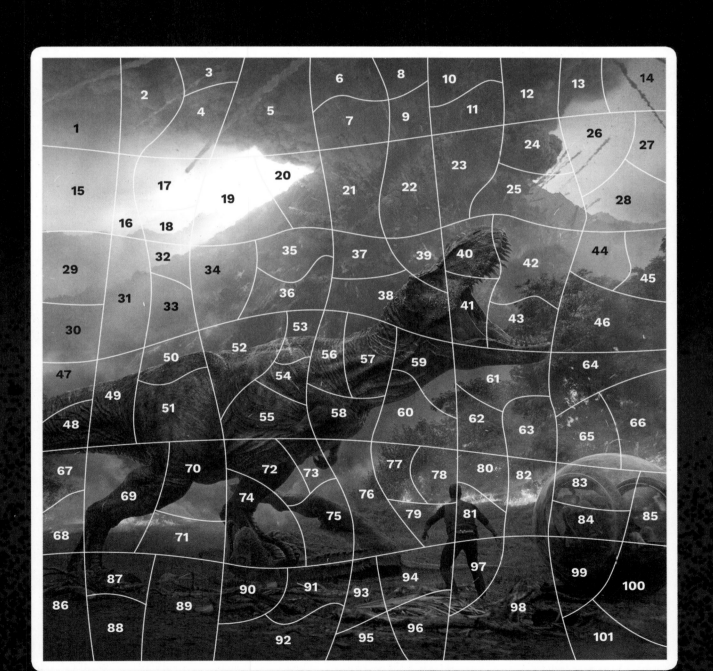

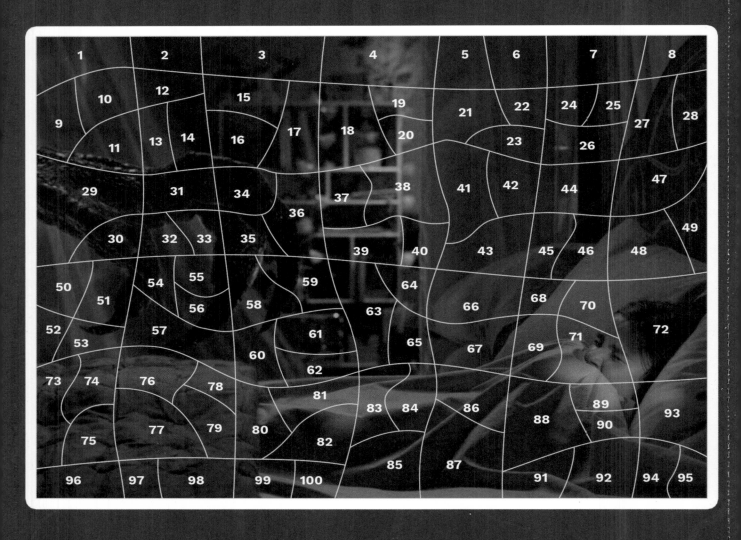

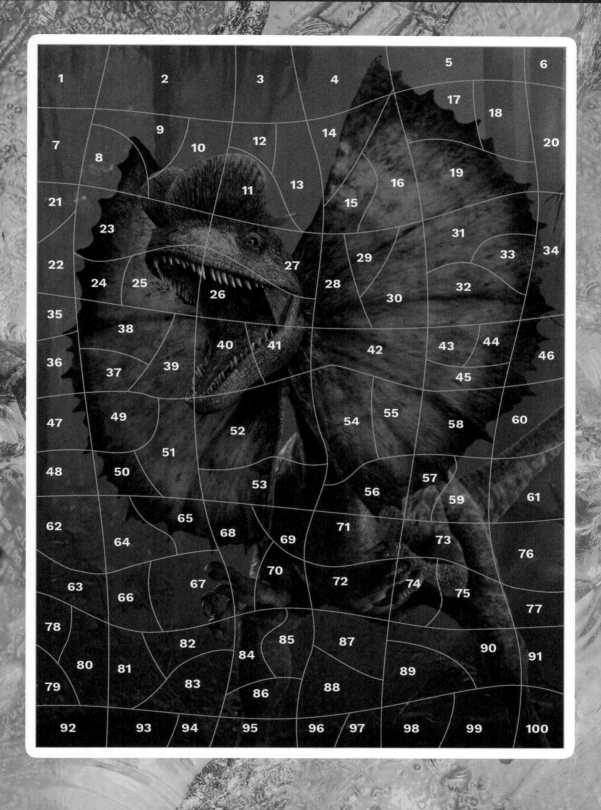

STICKERS

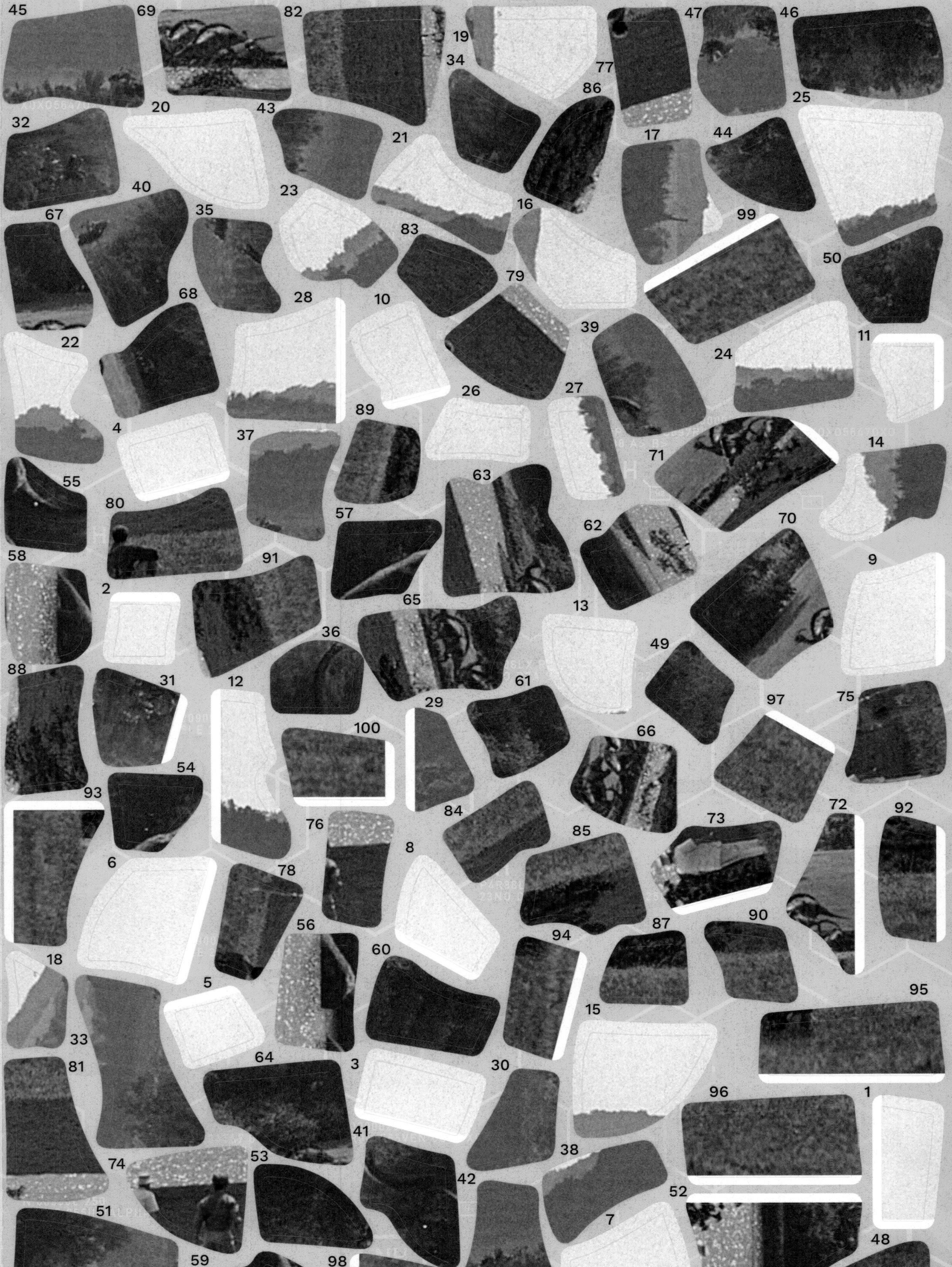

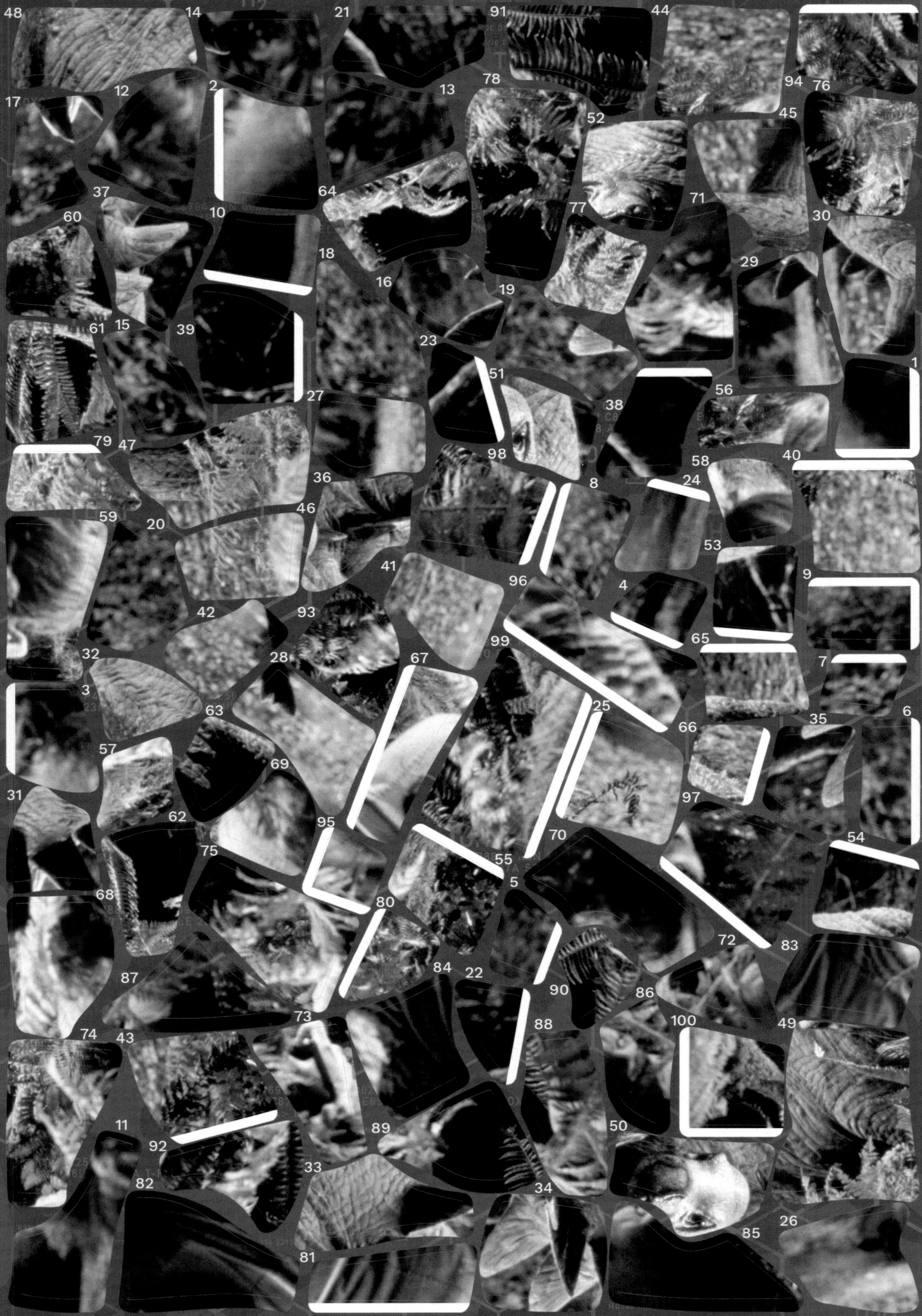

61

20
92
5
67
30
18
13
29
97
6
3
33
55
8
11
59
94
86
37
34
51
45
19
14
25
82
83
57
43
12
56
32
16
1
41
27
90
2
21
76
81
40
69
96
22
9
7
71
80
46
77
68
78
10
54
53
85
60
70
66
39
75
44
79
84
35
49
15
88
74
89
24
62
95
23
61
65
100
52
26
50
93
38
91
72
47
98
87
64
36
42
99
58
4
31
73
48
28
17
63

38
29
18
81
20
25
50
90
27
36
40
55
96
26
8
9
33
57
61
59
37
32
69
46
39
6
21
42
22
48
23
30
24
11
19
83
91
54
98
66
60
72
15
43
65
73
82
4
67
71
88
62
68
76
17
47
95
51
28
16
31
92
77
41
63
53
70
97
100
75
45
78
74
85
52
84
7
93
3
58
86
34
87
89
13
94
79
12
49
64
1
5
10
44
35
80
2
56
99
14

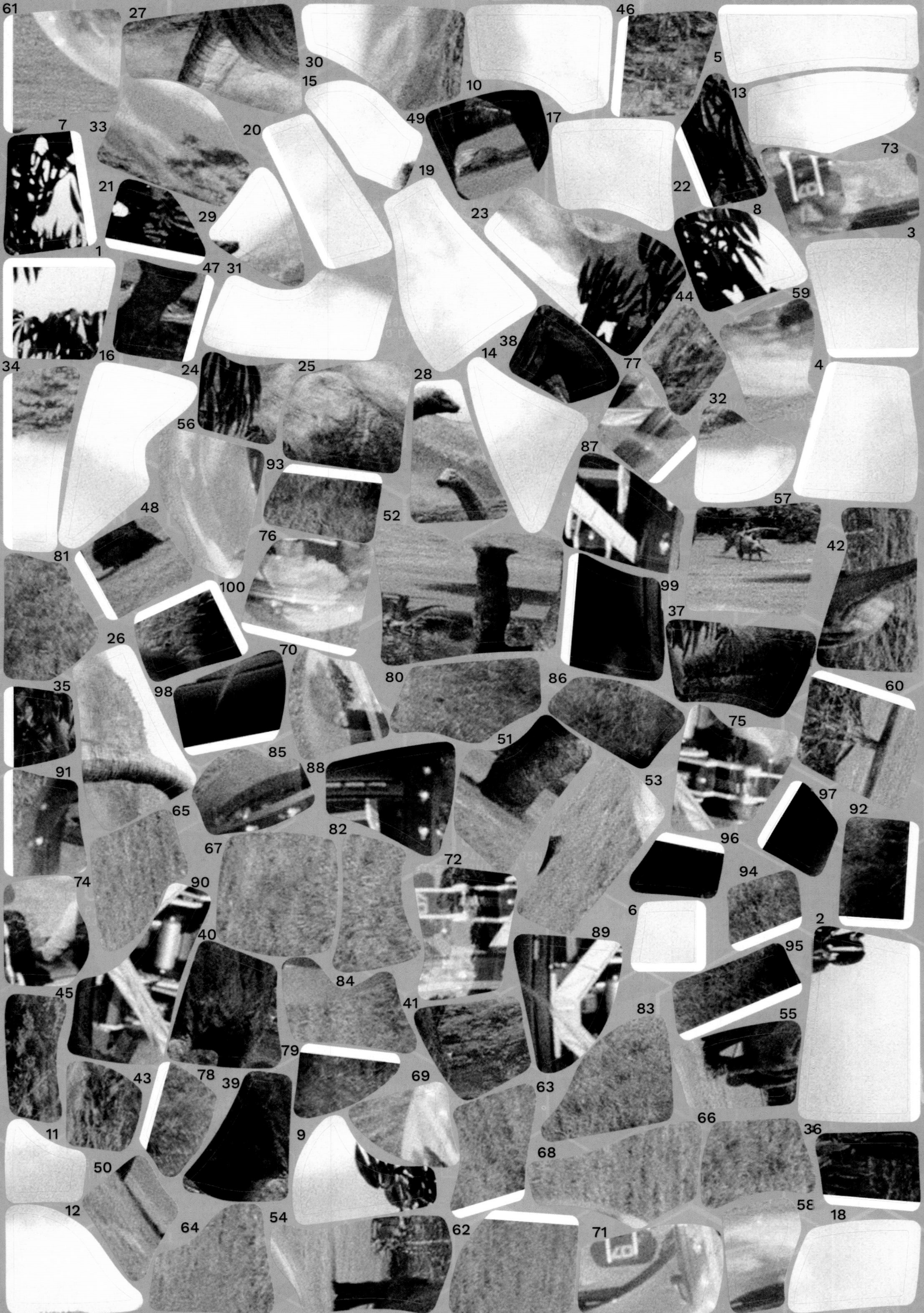

40
31
34
12
73
35
101
25
61
85
56
10
72
38
2
11
71
83
14
51
19
57
13
17
81
95
37
28
21
94
3
29
33
92
26
58
30
48
16
15
54
52
96
50
76
97
32
43
59
89
7
5
4
24
80
74
45
20
55
99
77
53
6
22
88
62
87
78
100
67
9
46
47
70
44
66
90
91
69
27
42
98
49
36
75
82
86
60
8
93
64
65
84
63
23
39
41
68
18
1
79

51 64 71 57 69
98 35 46 34
53 70 31 40
21 39 38 8
62 79 93 13
37 11 41
10 20 14 78 87
27 28 42
59 3 4 18 6 26 100
33 80 48 30 44
83 99 76 81 55
7 74 16 68 96
89 47 17 23 12
19 61 90
65 45 88 94
52 24 60 29
75 63 58 43
82 95 36 9
85 91 50 97 5
56 101 73 67 32
54 22 92 25 77
72 1 84 15 66
86 2 49

98
43
67
99
66
74
92
51
91
16
8
44
26
19
48
72
15
42
78
23
49
54
20
89
45
13
7
53
79
10
1
38
29
22
41
11
12
86
31
30
64
58
100
46
39
94
60
40
59
56
68
73
95
71
24
4
81
87
57
82
62
84
25
96
85
75
93
88
76
32
65
61
97
83
63
34
70
52
80
77
36
69
55
14
50
5
37
35
47
2
33
17
90
27
18
6
28
21
3
9

58
43
45
72
61
75
59
65
38
62
44
60
69
21
3
27
14
47
18
89
2
23
42
52
57
33
98
81
93
51
80
10
17
85
77
99
92
39
34
97
20
54
55
32
100
46
15
53
35
96
90
13
66
1
9
41
91
87
84
31
71
74
56
7
94
64
49
82
88
8
76
68
11
19
30
86
6
26
83
95
50
79
70
48
24
5
16
28
67
25
73
40
63
78
36
29
37
22
12
4

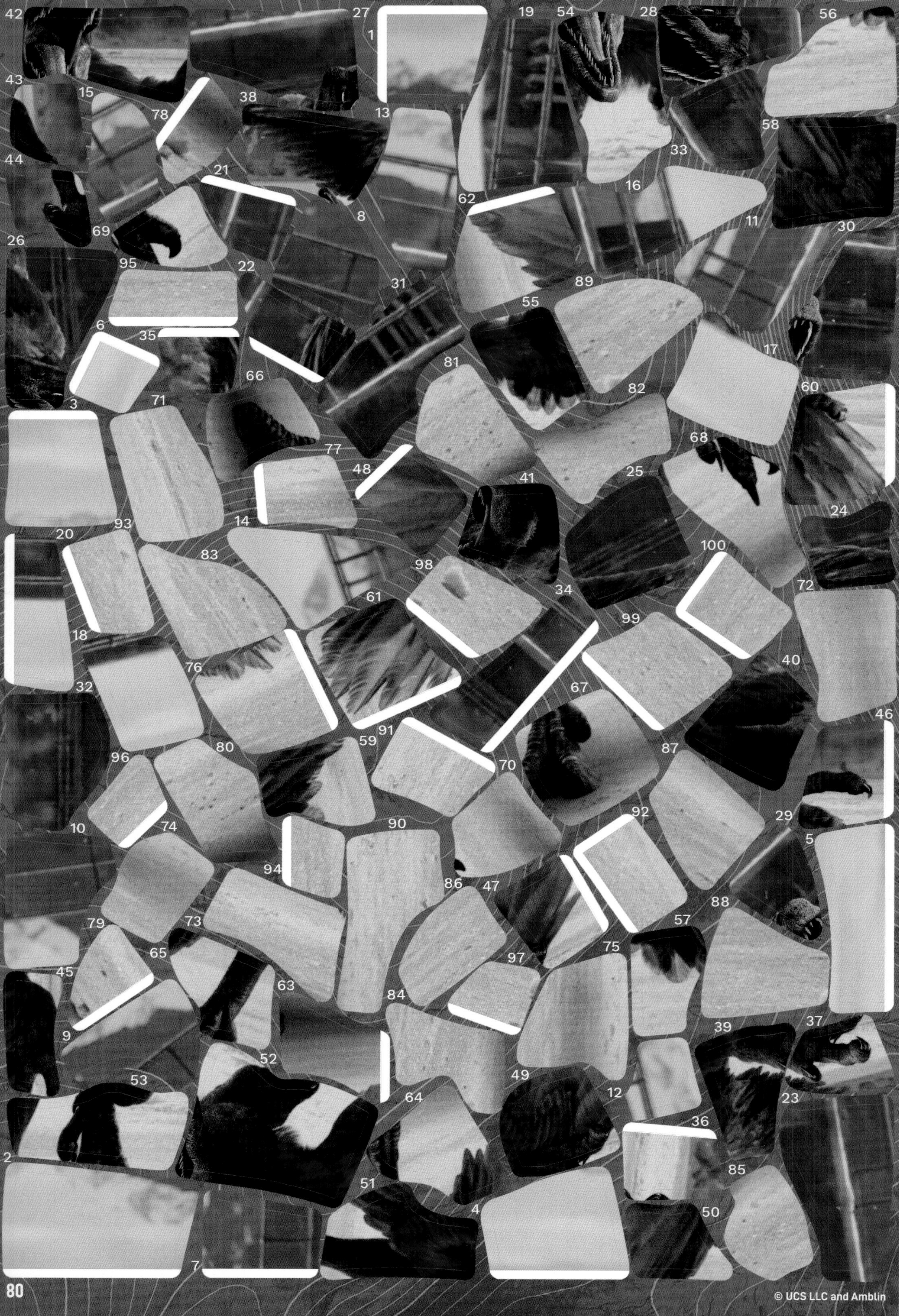